Ashes & Ambers

Ishika Chaterjee

BookLeaf Publishing

India | USA | UK

Made with ❤ on the BookLeaf Publishing Platform
www.bookleafpub.in
www.bookleafpub.com

Dedication

For the souls who are still hurting and healing—
Hold on, okay?
You'll grow out of this pain, I promise.
And until you do, I'm right here with you,
in every word, in every page.

Preface

Hey,

I'm Ishika, but you can call me Ish!

I'm your regular caffine addict, book hoarder, who went through a few sad chapters in real life and now working on the remission plot for the same.

If you're holding this book, I want you to know something—

you're not alone. Not in your heartbreak, not in your hurting, not in the way it lingers.

I wrote this because I've been there too.

Some nights felt endless. Some mornings, impossible.

But even in the darkest hours, something inside me whispered: *keep going.* This book is my whisper to you.

This book is me telling you that you're allowed to feel everything you feel.

I'm not going to tell you it's okay, or that you'll be okay anytime soon, because I know you won't. Not for a long time.

But what I will say is this: I'm sorry you had to feel this.

I'm sorry for the pain. I'm sorry for the root cause that took your smile away.

These poems aren't about pretending the hurt isn't there.
They're about sitting with it—holding it, letting it teach
you, and giving it space to soften over time.
They're about choosing yourself when nobody else does,
about being the love of your own life and loving yourself
extra hard on those damn gloomy days.
They're about the quiet moments between heartbreak
and healing—until the dawn finally shows up, and with
it, the first sunlight,and its warmth after what felt like an
endless hailstorm.

Note to Readers:
This collection spans through thoughts, emotions, and
experiences, blending personal reflections with a touch
of fiction—because let's face it, reality often needs a
creative twist to make it bearable.
While many pieces are rooted in my journey, others
come from the imaginative corners of my mind.
Together, they weave a narrative of growth, struggle, and
self-discovery.
That said, some parts of this book dive into sensitive and
challenging themes, including depression, grief, and
suicidal thoughts. These pieces are raw, honest, and
unfiltered, and they may be triggering for some readers.
Please approach them with care and take breaks if
needed.

If you're struggling or feel overwhelmed, know that you're not alone. Help is available, and reaching out is a brave and vital step. Below are some helplines in India where you can find support:

- AASRA: 91-9820466726 | Website: www.aasra.info
- Snehi: +91-9582208181 (9 AM to 9 PM)
- Vandrevala Foundation: 1860 266 2345 | 9999 666 555
- iCall: +91-9152987821 | Email: icall@tiss.edu

Remember, there's no shame in seeking help, and your feelings are valid. This book isn't just a collection of words—it's a conversation. And if these pages resonate with you, let them be a reminder that there's hope, healing, and light ahead.

With love,

Ish

Acknowledgements

I'd like to begin by expressing my gratitude and raising a toast to the incredible gang whose presence and support inspired me to write this.

To my mom — for being the fiercest fighter I know. You raised me with so much love, and even when things got messy, your love never wavered. Thank you for being my home.

To Sunidhi (Su)— my best friend, my constant. You stayed when I was a complete mess, when I was unbearable, when even I didn't want to deal with me. You've seen the ugliest parts of my story and never looked away. Thank you for loving me through it all.

To my Dadun — the coolest grandpa there ever is, and somehow the most excited teenager when it comes to my writings. Your pride lights up the whole room. Thank you for reading every word like it mattered—because to you, it always did.

To Shraddha (Ada) — for teaching me to love the moon and myself. For reminding me there's beauty even in the things that don't shine all the time.

To Swara —for treating me with unwavering love and kindness, never once making me feel weird—only seen.

To Dr. Nishu Joshi — thank you for sitting with my chaos, for letting me unravel one rant at a time. For hearing the pain between my words when I couldn't say it out loud to the world.

To Joe — for calling me out when I needed it most, and for being my favorite gossip partner. You've kept me grounded and real, and that means the world.

To Krish — for telling me not to quit, even when I wanted to throw the whole damn journey away. "Pause, but don't stop"—those words stayed. Thank you for hearing me even when I wasn't really speaking.

To Aditi — for being my first reader, for listening to every rushed piece of poetry, for cheering me on like it was your job, you helped me edit my half baked stories as my editor (even though I never paid you). You believed in these words and worlds when I didn't.

To my chaos crew—Oreo, Jerry, Tom, Kutkut, Muffin, Biscuit, and Tabby. You loved me without conditions. You licked my tears, curled up on my worst days, and reminded me what soft love feels like. I'd be lost without you.

To the people who broke me, bruised me, walked away, ghosted, lied, or made me question my worth—you gave me the pain that gave me these pages. So, thanks for the material.

To my readers — thank you for holding my heart in your hands, for finding pieces of your story in mine. If these words made you feel seen, less alone, or a little more understood— then every tear, every late night, every rewrite was worth it.
You are the reason I kept writing.

And lastly—
To me.
To the five-year-old Ish who dreamt way too big, talked way too loud, and refused to be quiet, no matter how much the world tried to shut her up. I'm proud of you. I love you
We made it to the pages.

CHEERS!!!

1. Left Alive

I'm broken in places no one can touch.
Not bruises, not scars—
just empty hollows where pieces of me used to live.

I scream without sound.
I cry without tears.
Even grief has grown tired of me.
I'm stuck in a dead end where the walls breathe despair,
and the ceiling hangs just low enough
to crush hope—but never kill it.

I am rotting in slow motion.
Suffocating in a life that refuses to end.
Death flirted, then left—
and now I'm trapped in the wreckage it forgot to finish.

People call it survival.
I call it cruelty.
Because I walk, talk, smile—
but I'm nothing.

Nothing but the aftermath.

And still—
no one notices the corpse
wearing my name.

2. Hell Loop

I wake up hurting.
I fall asleep hurting.
And in between, I convince myself I'm okay.
The pain doesn't change—
it just morphs,
a constant ache that never stops.
No beginning, no end,
just a deep, gnawing emptiness.
Some days, it whispers.
Most days, it screams.
But it never lets go.
I'm stuck in this hell loop of hurt—
trapped in the same bleeding grind,
too tired to fight,
too broken to find
any peace, any light,
just waiting for the next night.

3. I've got questions

Who do I tell, where do I go?
How do I grieve a love the world never knew?
The one I waited for, prayed for, bled for— was never
mine, but still shattered me.

How do I mourn what I never got to hold?
What do I do with all this love
that has nowhere to go but back into my own chest—
burning, screaming, silent.

To them, I was just a passing thing.
To me, you were everything.
A heartbeat I memorized.
A ghost I kept kissing in the dark.
You were never mine.

But God, I was yours.
Fully. Loudly. Quietly.
Utterly.

4. The Void

I howl at the void
and it spits my scream back in blood.
Not an echo—
a mutilation.
My pain returns sharper,
hungrier,
Like it's feeding on me.

I scream until my throat rips raw,
until silence feels like mercy.
But the void wants more.
It wants to break me
It wants to break more than just my bones

And I do.
I break in ways that aren't poetic.
I claw at my own chest,
trying to rip the ache out,
but it stays.
It always stays.

There is no healing here.
Only me,
on my knees,
begging a peace.

But the silence I get is the one
that keeps chewing
and chewing
and chewing
on what's left of me.

5. Have Mercy

Oh, grieve of mine, have mercy, please,
For I am lost in endless seas.
I bled for love, and bled for you,
And still, it's never far from view.

Each tear I shed, a shattered piece,
A quiet scream I can't release.
How long must I carry this pain inside,
Until I've drowned, or swallowed the tide?

6. You have got a friend in me

I befriended pain, it sat with me last night,
whispered softly, held me tight.
It coaxed me through the tears I couldn't hide,
and in its arms, I felt my heart collide.

It cried with me, not as a friend, but a lover—
each sob a reminder that I couldn't recover.
We sat in silence, two broken souls,
sharing the weight of what took its toll.

7. Shards and Thorns

I knew the heart to be made of tissues,
but why does mine feel like shattered, twisted issues?
Maybe it tried to garden a rose,
but all it found were thorns in its soul's repose.

It reached for beauty, thought it could bloom,
but it only welcomed pain into the room.
Now it's broken, jagged, and torn apart—
a heart that once loved, now lost in the dark.

8. Tea time

I called it high tea with Grief one day,
Dressed the table in the usual way.
Poured the tea with a practiced grace,
Wore my brightest, borrowed face.
We raised our cups with trembling hands,
She spoke in sighs I'd grown to understand.
My laughter cracked, the mask was brief—
Still, I played polite with Lady Grief.

9. Butterflies to Bones

You gave me butterflies,
then left me to cry.
Once I soared, now I fall,
an empty shell, no wings at all.
I held your love, soft and sweet,
now all I feel is bitter defeat.
From fluttering wings to brittle bones,
I rattle with echoes of you alone.

10. Promises Promises

"You Promised"
But you promised—
you promised you would not break me.
You held my trembling hands,
swore by the soft light between us,
whispered vows made of smoke and want.
You looked me in the eye,
steady and sure,
and told me I was safe.
But safety was a language
you never truly spoke.
You loved like a storm,
and I stood too close to the center.
You promised you would not break me—
but here I am,
picking up pieces
with bleeding hands,
learning that promises
are just softer ways to say goodbye.

11. Cry me a River of Sorrow

I cried me a river,
and drowned in sorrow's deep sea.
With hope lost to the current,
no wish to see what tomorrow could be.
The waves pulled me under,
far from the shore's embrace,
where light could never find me,
and I couldn't feel a trace.

12. Play date

I sat with Healing and Hurting by my side—
one held my hand, the other watched me cry.
Hurting spoke first, familiar and loud,
"Do you remember?" it asked,
and I nodded without pride.

Healing said nothing, just offered a breath,
a silence that didn't ache like death.
Hurting pointed to scars and opened old doors,
while Healing stitched threads
through invisible sores.

They didn't fight.
They didn't need to.
One reminded me of what was lost,
the other of what I still had to grow into.

I poured tea for them both
and let the night pass slow.
Because sometimes, to heal,

you must sit with what hurts—
and not run when it starts to show.
15

13. Favour Turned in

You broke me—loud, cruel, and proud.
Shattered me like glass just to watch me bleed.
I begged in whispers; you answered with silence.
Loved you soft, and you loved me to death.

Now I've burned what's left of you in me.
And suddenly, *you're* the one who's hurting?
Don't cry now—
this is just your echo coming home.

14. Before Spring, There Was Winter

Before I met spring, I met winter's bite,
Cold, dark days that swallowed the light.
I shivered through nights with no warmth to find,
Frozen in silence, with a heart left behind.
The winds howled, the snow fell deep,
I buried my hopes in the ground I couldn't keep.
But before I could thaw, before I could sing,
I had to endure the pain winter would bring.

15. Idiot

Today I smiled, then snorted loud,
then cackled like a girl unbowed.
At the fool I was, so blind, so true—
loving enough for me and you.
I held it all while you let go,
clung to hope you'd never show.
What a joke, and now I see—
the punchline, love, was always me.

16. Cross roads

Maybe that's where I went wrong —
You craved the warmth, I craved the belong.
You wanted fire to keep you near,
I wanted walls to hold you here.
And in the end, we both let go,
Of something neither dared to show.
Left with the ashes, cold and bare,
Of what we were — or never were there.

17. I am the Sun

You were never the sun — I was.
I lit the sky without a pause.
But loving you, I dimmed my light,
Mistook your shadow for my night.

I burned for you, then came undone,
Forgot that I was always the sun.
You never shone — you only caught
The glow I gave... and I forgot

18. Love confession of Pain

I asked Pain, now a dear friend of mine —
What if I gave in? What if this is the end?
It looked at me like a lover once scorned,
With eyes that whispered, you're the only one I've
mourned.
And in its gaze, so hollow, so long—
I saw it ache to keep me, as if I belong.

With a sigh Pain said
If you ever left,
not that you would,
not that the stars would dare let you go—
but if you did,
I'd weave your name into the wind,
so the world still hums your song.

I'd press your laughter into the earth,
let flowers rise where your footsteps once danced,
so even the ground remembers
how you made it feel less alone.

I'd gather your words,
each aching, burning, beautiful verse,
and scatter them like constellations,
so when someone looks up, lost,
they find you shining back.

But you are here, and still you breathe,
Through aching nights and silent grief.
I will not pen your final page,
Your tale's too wild to cage with age.

The stars don't set—they only roam,
And even lost hearts find their home.
You're not a chapter meant to close,
You are the story—The one I'd watch as it grows.

19. Here

I will get there —
one day.
But right now,
at this moment,
I am *here*.
And the last version of me,
the broken one,
the gasping one,
couldn't even fathom
the thought of standing here,
breathing here,
living here.
She didn't believe
she would survive the fall.
She couldn't see
this small, stubborn hope growing in the cracks.
But I'm here.
And that is enough.
For now,
it is everything.

20. I met love today

I met love again—
it no longer looked like you.

It looked like my mother's smile,
soft and warm like the morning dew.
It looked like my dog's snug,
her fur a comfort on the hardest days,
and my best friends, laughing over brunches,
with a pint of chocolate chip ice cream to share.

It looked like coffee at dawn,
from the corner café, as the sun kissed the sky.
It looked like the flowers blooming
on my window sill, reaching up high.

I met love in the traffic,
between honking cars and hurried feet,
in the tabby cat on the sidewalk,
and the old couple I helped cross the street.

It looked like the reflection in the mirror,
a girl smiling back, no longer hurt.
25

Love looks so different now—
familiar, but fresh, like the world reborn,
and for the first time, I see it clearly—
love's been here all along, since the dawn.

21. Happily never after

Maybe my happy ending
was never with you.
Maybe it was always meant to be with me —
with choosing kindness for myself,
with choosing softness that didn't bleed me dry.
Maybe it was in being myself,
without bending,
without breaking,
without becoming the heartbreaker
you taught me to be,
the one who shattered more than just my own heart.
Maybe survival was the ending.
Maybe loving myself,
even after you,
was the story I was meant to write all along.